Morel Mushroom

Hunting My Way

BRYAN "GRIZ" FEISEL

PAGE PUBLISHING
Conneaut Lake, PA

First originally published by Page Publishing 2023

ISBN 979-8-88960-627-7 (pbk)
ISBN 979-8-88960-638-3 (digital)

Printed in the United States of America

C o n t e n t s

Foreword

Morel Mushroom Hunting My Way is an insightful basic guide that focuses on both the how-to and the simple joy of morel hunting. Bryan blazes a proven path to success by sharing both the basics and the subtleties of his craft. In the twenty-plus years I have known Bryan, I've come to appreciate his incredible passion for the outdoors, and especially, his use of outdoor adventure to cultivate lasting friendships. He has a guide's mentality, focused on delivering enjoyment of the experience. Both the hunt and the ensuing culinary festivities are equally treasured ("livin' large!" as Bryan would say). For Bryan, outdoor pursuits are not simply recreation but a way of life.

Morels are highly prized, but often an enigma to the inexperienced. Hidden behind Bryan's seemingly simple go-to methods are years of observations, meticulous records, and a thirst and willingness to always learn more. For Bryan, "my way" isn't "my way or the highway"—it's a reliable process that he constantly refines. Bryan and I never run out of new questions and theories about mysterious morels. Good luck and happy hunting! *Morel Mushroom Hunting My Way* will give you the motivation, confidence, and knowledge to become a successful morel hunter.

—Kent Budd, expert mycologist and morel hunter

Introduction

When I think of morel mushroom hunting, it conjures up memories in the mid-1960s, walking the slopes of Sioux City, Iowa, with my father, Richard C. Feisel. You see, Dutch Elm disease had just occurred, and mushrooms were quite abundant! It was not uncommon to haul grocery bags of them away from the newly dead elms.

Dad would begin the season on the south slopes and finish up four weeks later on the north slopes. I ate so many mushrooms one time, I got sick of eating too many. I could not look at a morel for the next thirty years. I picked up hunting them again in the nineties and have become an expert on the subject. I begin the season here in central western Wisconsin in late April looking for tiny morels called micros. This is the second in the My Way book series and will bring you on a venture into the world of nature at its best. This is morel mushroom hunting my way!

C h a p t e r   1

The Basics—Only a Start

When most people think of morels, they think of dead elms. Back to them in a minute. I have found a better tree—dying cottonwoods. They start earlier, produce longer, and produce more mushrooms. They are gold mines in the morel world.

When an experienced mushroom hunter walks in the woods, they look at the trees, not the ground. They look for peeling bark. They identify if it is an elm or a cottonwood. Once found and identified, they walk to the base of the so-called target. Most times, there will be nothing because the morels haven't fruited yet, or the tree will not produce for whatever reason. This continues throughout the hunt.

As the season goes on, more trees are checked, more ground, and hopefully more morels are found. As far as terrain, my favorite is river bottoms—my mainstay. They heat up quicker, hold tons of moisture, and cottonwoods are usually in river bottoms. I also hunt southwest slopes early in the season—they get the most sun! They are the main producers if the trees are there. I progress to the south slopes midseason—again, lots of sun. I end my season on the north slopes, and I can tell by the trees when the fat lady is ready to sing.

Elms: I prefer twelve inches diameter and above. I don't mess with small trees—usually only a couple mushrooms by them. I am after quantity and high efficiency of my time. Big elms mean more morels.

Cottonwoods: My brother-in-law, Ken, lost a big cottonwood tree from a storm. He and his family harvested tons of morels over the next three years by the stump. Cottonwoods are my preferred tree, and few know about them unless they stumble upon them. I seek them out.

Figure 1. Author overlooking a prime river bottom.

C h a p t e r   2

Micros and the Early Season

Ramps are the first plants noticeably to emerge—sometime in early April in central western Wisconsin (see figure 2). Where legal, they are good to harvest and eat as well. They are like a green onion to me.

It's mid-April now, and I already have several targets identified. In the river bottoms and southwest slopes, I begin finding tiny morels called micros by dead elms and dying cottonwoods. These morels are tiny and challenging to find (see figure 4). In your favor is the fact the understory has not grown yet helping you to see them.

These morels are usually bug free and very clean. They are my favorites. I like the challenge of finding them and eating them fresh.

Figure 2. Ramps, basically wild green onions, are an early indicator that the season is progressing. This photo was taken April 14 in central western Wisconsin.

Figure 3. Another good view of the river bottoms the author likes to hunt.

Figure 4. The first micros of the season. Always welcome.

Figure 5. The author found micros by this elm.

Figure 6. The author with a nice mess of micros.

Chapter 3

A Typical Day Hunting Morels

Okay, targets have been identified in the areas you plan to hunt. If someone is with me, as they often are, I make sure they know about protecting themselves from insects and nasty plants (see chapter 5). In figure 7, one of my hunting friends is standing by a fruiting tree. Notice he is wearing red—this is nice because I can see where he is at. The other approach with experienced hunters is to wear camo and go incognito, thus protecting your spots and targets.

Once at the spot, I might park the truck far away and walk up to the spot. As stated earlier, I scan the woods for dead trees, and if I find new ones, walk to the base checking for morels. Then I hit known targets. I have found that every two days is a good rhythm to recheck known targets. Introducing new friends is a fun way to go (see figure 8).

The amount of time you have determines how many areas and targets you can hit. Sometimes we travel to southeast Minnesota or Iowa and hunt all day or several days. One dying cottonwood (see figure 9) produced for nine years and over five hundred morels. Take new paths every day when checking known targets as you may find new ones.

When the hunt is over, we usually sit at a table and divide the morels (see figure 10). If I am not going to eat them right away, I store them in the fridge in a paper bag. They can last, say five days that way. The payoff for the day is usually morels in the pan (see figure 11).

Figure 7. Hunting buddy Phil Soo
standing by a fruiting tree.

Figure 9. This now dead cottonwood produced over five hundred morels over a nine-year period.

Figure 10. The morels get bigger midseason.
Here is Garth Christensen with a mess.

Figure 11. The payoff—mushrooms in the pan.

Chapter 4

Targets

Elms: When anyone thinks of morel trees, they think of elms. The staple is dying elms! Bark freshly peeling, still holding bark and not bald, white all around the tree.

Cottonwoods: As stated earlier, this is the my staple. I seek them out because they produce for several years.

Miscellaneous targets: Apple trees, especially in old orchards can be good. Lawns—more than once, I have found morels in lawns with no tree targets. Sad to say, most people mow them under.

One time, Kent Budd (see foreword) and I were hunting in southeast Minnesota. Kent found a single morel by an oak tree. He and I were both surprised and looked for an elm tree nearby. We never found one! Live oaks can produce, but the odds are much lower than for dead elms.

Finally, I called a ranger station further north in Wisconsin to keep my season extended. He said they find the morels by dying ash in the Chequamegon National Forest.

Figure 12. The author by a prime elm target. We sometimes couple the morel hunt with stream fishing.

Figure 13. Another prime elm target.

Figure 14. Excellent peeling bark on an elm
in the ideal state of decomposition.

Figure 15. This morel and about one
hundred others were found.

Figure 16. This elm target. Damaged during a tornado.

Figure 17. Same elm as figure 16. Notice
morel is growing at right angle to the tree.

Figure 18. Fellow hunter Laura Stilp with over six pounds of morels, found in tornado-hit area!

Figure 19. Helping young people identify targets is key to keeping the sport going. Austyn Stilp here with her first two morels ever found on her own.

Figure 20. Everyone, including those with four paws, want in on the action. Austyn Stilp, Roxy, and the author.

Figure 21. Tyler Still with a big morel! He was our "bigfoot" man last year.

Figure 22. Now that is a morning's work.
Over seven pounds! Cory Stilp.

Figure 23. Good-looking elm target.

Figure 24. Youngsters on the hunt!

Figure 25. A bonus. Fawn white-tailed deer. *Never* approach. Take photo from where you see it.

Chapter 5

Insect and Nasty Plant Prevention

In the early season and mainly throughout, ticks are the number 1 concern. Here in western central Wisconsin, we have deer ticks and plenty of them. I had a bad case of Lyme disease back in the mid-eighties and had to be hospitalized twice! Don't throw caution to the wind.

Here's what we do: wear coveralls soaked in a liquid spray containing permethrin. DEET is good, but permethrin is better. We then tuck the bottoms into above ankle rubber boots and spray them also. Treat the coveralls and leave them in the garage or wherever for several days once treated properly. Also, a hat is a must. The boots should be sprayed every time out. I wear latex rubber gloves when spraying. You do not want chemicals on your skin.

Mosquitoes: Late season they are prevalent. Wear a head net and stay away from sprays on your skin. These pests make hunting difficult, and I am glad the season is almost over by then.

Nasty plants: Poison ivy, nettles, itch weed, and the like are out. The old saying "leaves of three, let 'em be" holds true! Also I wear a light leather glove to prevent scratches from buckthorn and prickly ash, etc.

When you get home, take the coveralls off in the garage or outside. Strip down and go immediately to take a shower.

I also pick ticks off as I go, just throwing them in the woods.

Figure 26A. Plants you want to have around
are may apples and flowering plants.

Figure 26B. Most flowering plants are safe and make for good understory, keeping the morels cool.

Chapter 6

After the Hunt

Okay, you have a nice mess of morels, and you are home. Morels are either yellow, gray, or black (rarely do I find these; see figure 27). The first thing we do if we are in a group is divide them among the hunters.

Next, I take mine and go to the kitchen. If I am going to store any, as stated earlier, I keep them up to five days in a brown paper bag.

The ones I will eat, I put in a large bowl of water, add one tablespoon salt, and spin them. I dump the first and repeat the process with fresh water. Next, I slice the morel in half lengthwise and clean out any bugs. If the morels are from gritty soil, I take the sprayer with cold water and give some good shots on the fold side.

Finally, I place them fold side down on paper towels to release any excess moisture. The morels are now ready for any recipe, including those attached in this book. I also bread, season, and fry in real butter for side dishes. One more thing I do and love them is add them to scrambled eggs (see figure 29). Morels should be sautéed first, and a good rule of thumb is always make sure you cook them at least seven minutes unless the recipe specifies differently.

Figure 27. A nice mix of yellows and grays.

Figure 28. The author found these morels in
one hour at two new trees. Ready to clean.

Figure 29. Two medium-sized yellows. The author might clean and put these in his scrambled eggs.

Figure 30. Kent Budd with a few
morels from a local spot.

Recipes

Angel Morels

Ingredients:

    1/3 c diced onion (Vidalia preferred)
    4 tbsp butter
    1/3 c diced red pepper
    1 lb. fresh Morels, sliced vertically
    2 tbsp flour
    1 tsp salt
    1 tsp sugar
    1 tbsp soy sauce
    1/2 lb. angel hair pasta

Instructions:

Prepare the pasta according to the directions and drain. In a large pan, sauté pepper and onion in 2 tablespoons butter for 1 minute. Make a roux out of the flour, soy sauce, and sugar in a separate pan (it has to be stirred constantly). Turn heat on low. Add morels, onion, and pepper mixture. Cover and cook for 30 minutes. Serve over pasta. Enjoy.

Stuffed Mushroom Caps

Ingredients:

1 lb. morel mushrooms
3 tbsp grated Parmesan cheese
2 garlic cloves
1 onion, minced
1 c fine breadcrumbs
1 tbsp chopped fresh parsley
2 tbsp butter, melted
Salt and pepper to taste
6 tbsp olive oil

Instructions:

Remove the stems from the mushrooms; mince the stems. Mix the Parmesan cheese, garlic, parsley, and melted butter thoroughly. Add chopped mushroom stems. Season with salt and pepper.

Stuff the caps with the filling. Place 2 tablespoons of the olive oil in shallow baking pan. Place the stuffed caps in the pan and drizzle the remaining olive oil over the top of the mushrooms.

Bake in a preheated oven at 400 degrees F for 25 minutes or until brown and crisp. Serve with a red wine. Enjoy.

Tenderloin in Morel Sauce

Ingredients:

2 to 3 tbsp olive oil
4 filet mignon of venison, elk or bison
Salt and pepper
4 to 6 minced shallots
3 tbsp butter
2 garlic cloves, minced
1 lb. fresh morels split in half
1/2 c brandy
1 c red wine
1 c beef stock
1 tbsp fresh chopped thyme
1 tbsp fresh chopped parsley or chives to garnish

Preparation:

Meat: Rub olive oil all over the meat. Sprinkle with salt and pepper. Set aside. Grill each side for 3 to 5 minutes over high heat for rare to medium rare. Turn meat only once. You don't want this dish beyond medium.

Sauce: Sauté shallots in 2 tablespoons butter over medium heat until they begin to turn brown. Add garlic and morels. Sauté for 2 minutes.

Add brandy. Increase heat to high. When most of the liquid is evaporated, add wine. Repeat evaporation process. When about 2/3 of the wine has evaporated, add stock and thyme. Reduce whole mixture by half. Turn off heat. When sauce stops boiling, add 1 tablespoon butter. Season with salt and pepper. Serve over meat at once. Garnish with parsley or chives.

Serve with a good red wine. Enjoy.

Epilogue

Well, there you have it, that's *Morel Hunting My Way*. I hope you've enjoyed this adventure as much as I and my hunting comrades have. It's a fun sport, challenging and always with something more to learn. My tactics are proven. Employ them. I wish you the best in the woods, and remember, don't look at the ground until you find a target!

May you always have lots of rain, sunshine, and morels at the base of a tree. Good luck hunting for the mighty morel.

About the Author

Bryan "Griz" Feisel has developed a passion and has a knack for hunting morel mushrooms. Bryan began hunting with his father, Richard C. Feisel, on the slopes around Sioux City, Iowa.

After a thirty-year hiatus, Bryan picked up the sport again in west central Wisconsin and trips back to Iowa. This is the second in the My Way series of books.

Bryan lives in west central Wisconsin and is an accomplished author, photographer, inventor, and a self-taught naturalist. Bryan owns his own company, Feisel's Outdoors, and also guides for hunting and fishing (for free). He loves to introduce people to hunting morels. Notice all the people in this book have big smiles on their faces. There's something about this small mushroom that people just adore.

Bryan volunteers over 140 hours per year at the Minnesota Humane Society where he adopts out felines and canines.

Bryan calls the morels his "beauties" and hopes you learned something from this book.